Remarriages

Robin Wyatt Dunn

Scarlet Leaf

2017

Robin Wyatt Dunn - Remarriages

Robin Wyatt Dunn - Remarriages

© 2017 by Robin Wyatt Dunn

All rights reserved. No part of this book may be reproduced, stored in a retrieval system or transmitted in any form or by any means without the prior written permission of the publishers, except by a reviewer who may quote brief passages in a review to be printed in a newspaper, magazine or journal.

All poems in this book have been left as the author intended.

Scarlet Leaf Publishing House has allowed this work to remain exactly as the author intended.

ISBN: 978-1-988827-45-2

PUBLISHED BY SCARLET LEAF

Toronto, Canada

Robin Wyatt Dunn - Remarriages

Robin Wyatt Dunn - Remarriages

it's underneath everything
each moment
barnacles scraping the sky
you and I mirrors of the void

hold me tight for the star
and for the dart over the board
hold me tight for the sword
at my throat
and hold me tight
for the entropy within my bark

over the night

give me everything
the sky
and the void
give me the truth

Robin Wyatt Dunn - Remarriages

these days it's hard to make a living
hard to make a killing even
everyone keeps crawling out of the
grave
stumbling drunk
and pissed off
unable to find a doctor or a home

me, I keep fighting the good fight
with the coffee percolator
putting it in
turning it on
and watching the water quality drop

me, I keep my eye on the sky
where we have written clouds

these words are gods,
small and delightful
agents from another planet
planet history
planet quark
whose mustard gas is a mild fart
whose righteousness is only mild
indigestion
and whose rutabagas shine in the sun

Robin Wyatt Dunn - Remarriages

come in to the shadow of my evening
glasses
we are making coffee

this tree is my friend

Robin Wyatt Dunn - Remarriages

it's enough
the stalwart weight of my bones
and the sound of talking
some startled
some weeping
some laughing
in the evening

when I was a boy voices were like
planets
moving over my head

now they are like birds
on my shoulders

Robin Wyatt Dunn - Remarriages

these times fall over my head
in encephalitic bliss
slow and fine
tinkling wine
a sledgehammer made out of years

place the rack back on the bun
and sun the fanny till it's done
she's got a lot to let out
from her gout
and her earnest narrative
of the people's escape from slavery

these times imprison well
with the ludicrous swell of the gun of
the stars
firing the earth into space

firing the brain to the hands
firing the words to the year

Robin Wyatt Dunn - Remarriages

Now, I must lie to you
Though the lie is also the truth.

The limits of my range are showing
Forty meters hereabouts
A certain oven
Overhang
Strand of trees
Some water
The chipmunk.

No one hereabouts hovers right
On the right side
Near the exit
From the cave

It's all one thing, of course
I'd be lying--and I am--
If I said there were clear distinctions
Marks on the path to tell you where
to go
A feeling in the bones to mark the
perturbation
In the stillness of thought
But still:

Haven't you seen me somewhere
before?

I thought I knew you too
When I saw you walking.

Robin Wyatt Dunn - Remarriages

so shine me on
in this bare moonlight
whose essence is the sun
over you
and in your eyes

shine me on over the dark
whose essence is your soul
liquid and fire
rambunctious and afraid

shine me on into the fire
whose name is my own
older than me
older than the rocks

each life makes a heart
whose circumference circles the void
steepled and shaped over the aeon
ravaged cursus of you
whose hue rouges the lime light
of yous
prosody or war
striking the tent
and moving over the light

Robin Wyatt Dunn - Remarriages

Prison, prison, prison
Prisoner, prisoner

Prison my prisoner

My prisoner

Prisoner!

Prison once meant "prize"

Hold it in your hands

This beautiful thing

Shiny
Noble
Astonishing
Concrete and blood

This prize
Earns rewards
Earns friends

It keeps you awake at night

it sleeps under your bed

Robin Wyatt Dunn - Remarriages

It marches centuries
like water

This prize

Beacons
This mark
over your eye

I am your prisoner

I am your prison

the right goes up and down
spinning thread
making sounds

over my back, fine wires sketch other
sounds:
years and years.

Everything I want is far away,
And all that's near is so dear I fear it;
Why should I love these simple
things
so easily taken away?

What is it I've been listening to,
Since I was a boy?

Robin Wyatt Dunn - Remarriages

bent right our reaver smokes the
grave
craving gravity
some theater
or the nearness of now
some headache or music
the bastion of the sky
flirting with events
rash and diligent
exploding colors over the mast of the
forest

whose barren burden
deer
or birds
blacken the midnight of their passing
enrichment inside the snow-filled
winter
filled with the blessing of agony

minutes mirror over the roof
where he stares at me
ears flipping

our reaver banes and bones the back
and brain
bullets and graves

pull the curtain and declare the voice
god
and your arms props

run into the snow

For Roberto Bolano

Poets chew on my balls
And climb over my back
Swing from my hair
Dangle over my grave.

The poets are watching the sky
To see what is written on it
And they are playing basketball, with a telephone.

Poets have come over to stay in my house.
They have found the food, and are cooking it, on the roof.
They will not give me any of it.
Also, they are reading my books and are complaining.

The poets are angry about reality
It is not conforming to their expectations.
Some of them make love in the doorway,
To prove that reality is wrong.

Robin Wyatt Dunn - Remarriages

One of them is beautiful, a woman.
She will not look at me.

Over in the clouds the poets have
parked a judicial system
Complete with a god and a justice of
the peace
But no jail
They take turns being the prosecutor
and the convicted
Wearing the haloes.

In the kitchen,
They have begun to smoke
marihuana,
And talk about sunsets.
Sunsets are boring, they say.
And they nod, sagely.

I do not want to say goodbye to the
poets so I invite them to stay at my
house, even though we have run out
of food.

The socialists have pointed out that
the state should have provided food
for us; most of us agree except for
Jose, who points out it is immoral to
eat food. We agree with him also.

Outside, it has begun to rain,
And we are sad.
There is no sadness like the sadness
of rain.
Like the sadness of their faces, in
marble.
Thieves before the execution,
laughing.

Robin Wyatt Dunn - Remarriages

each light makes a spark
in the light
where it existed
where it is thinking about existing

each spark makes a light
inside the space where you are
sleeping

- -

*"each light makes a spark" first appeared
at Duane's PoeTree blog, Jan. 25, 2017.*

Death to California, USA
Death to the Caliph
The Successor
Death to Sacramento, and Los
Angeles
Death to all of the Angels
And their Gods

Death to Turtle Island

Death to all the names

Death to the King

Hold his head in your mind

Over the precipice

The people are rejoicing

In his blood

Death to the idea of the idea

Death to the trajectory and the orbit

Death to the hurry and the wash

Death to the flag

Ride the bear

To the bonfire

Robin Wyatt Dunn - Remarriages

My friend loves me
In fire;

No telling when
What bend
Or insist
His wrist
Or the bark
Or the bank

the end
the turf

what worth is the human soul
so tired

mystical
and fragrant with god
with the truth

whose agency ignites my spirit
over this pedestrian park?

imagined and nightmarish
impossible to imagine

his love binds me to the earth
who is only a servant of higher things

Robin Wyatt Dunn - Remarriages

whose mind is the febrile corner of
the stars
whose dance

makes me dance

my friend dances too
like a bad actor
like a haunted house
coursing over the mind of a cinema-
addict
drunk and happy

it is all right to know nothing
of what came before
in evenings like this
because
well, because
it just is

and your friend is back

leering and elegant
a full sport
in a dignified failure
of a nation.

the full value

of a huge equation
spilling its variables over the paper
over the chalkboard
over the university
igniting the library
with sex
and footsteps

each luminary descends
Homer
and Faulkner

to remind us to keep quiet
before the book
and the water

but Bobby is still singing
because he is happy

Robin Wyatt Dunn - Remarriages

beat down the grum
who suns the dome of your hearsay

who opens the tome of your caress
who burns the name of your regret

who loves you

it's time:
stunning and bright
limning your body with fire

it's no hero
nor light
this piano music reminds me of the
flapjack kids and they were nice kids
but they had murder in their eyes
there in the Nevada desert where
murders go to sleep and where
countries go to die, and this beauty
speaks like triumph over the sea,
whose name is my own, yes, it's my
own, and it can be yours too, if you'll
follow me, like Jesus but without the
child rape, or child porn, just this old
piano:

whose stellar music gravity swarms
the nation
lighting up old bars
and the eyes of old men
whose justice is an old shoe
whose mind is a barley hole
whose fingers stump sockets
whose beards terrify old women
whose balls swing over the ocean

we ignite
we unite
over the death of America

Robin Wyatt Dunn - Remarriages

over the death of the world
old and new
to burn this life
in arizona
in Timbuktu

and in you

this lightning deserves no other
reward
than an A flat
or a C minus
meditating on the grilled cheese
sandwich and pickle
still waiting at the diner

Mr. American Man

Mr. American Man
Whose Voice Did You Wear?
Who Did Your Hair?
Whose Love Was Yours?
Whose Cathedral Did You grace?

And What Cities Did You Bomb?
Did you love each city that you
bombed?

Will you bomb us too?
With your big balls?

American Man?

In this waltz,
Where we have set music,
The United Nations (your invention!)
Are playing
the tuba
And the violin

For your dance steps

1 2 3

1 2 3

Robin Wyatt Dunn - Remarriages

Around and around
with the champagne

Made in Nevada
Nuclear

We are happy to have you here
American Man

And we are ready to get Jiggy With It

because Jiggy Has Been Without it
For Too Long

And in Reuniting Jiggy With It
We Hope to be Reunited With You
Too

With the Cheetos
And the hairdressers

And the long nights and stars

And the harmonica

This one is for you,
American Man,
With beans.

Robin Wyatt Dunn - Remarriages

Rud the rudder
Hum the hummer
Chant the chartreuse sibilance a knife
A pike
Pray and spike the mist over your
face
It's beautiful

Life and religion inside the i-phone
Penetrable
A parking meter selling C4
for the aftermath of nations:

Cheat me well and easy
On the Parkay floor
And I'll send you the right ones and
zeroes
For your own personal revelation:

At the end of a long night
Before you get your door open

Robin Wyatt Dunn - Remarriages

it's no accident
nor any regret
at the low time of the evening
when everything is slow
and the fog has lifted
and the stars come out

no one will remember
how you were that night
except for you

Robin Wyatt Dunn - Remarriages

pen paper and sex
hold still and undress
scent the air and stifle the laugh
over the draft of your hair

enrapture this cocoon of love
for your esquire

in the mire of love
in the bonny heat

whose ray absconds the periphery
with your embrace

jackboots and eyes
over your desire

Have you seen the country

witch away all of the fluff
your duff she burns and I hear it in
my sleep

well, it's after that now
but I can still hear it.

Have you seen the country?
Who we have been?
And who we are now?
Maybe you haven't seen?
Or seen, and not wanted to.

I think I'm not seeing it, or maybe,
that I have seen it, and will not again,
that what I saw was some other
country, that I remember, from a
story.

Some other life.

But which one is this one?

- -

"Have you seen the country" first appeared in 1947 Journal, Feb. 8, 2017.

Robin Wyatt Dunn - Remarriages

The world is ending every day
Today, the world is ending

You are ending today
Put down your final words
and close the book
Turn off the TV
Go to sleep

and dream:

the world is ending today
in beautiful color
streaming starlight
a comet
or a politician
a politician comet!
streaking over the fight

of delight

the world ends today
in my song
and what's wrong
and what's for

on your before

before I ask

was it you who said

I was beautiful?

this song is what for
now ending
again
and again
and again

Robin Wyatt Dunn - Remarriages

I can't leave you now
because you broke me in
like a city you used to wear
and then forgot about
but it keeps pouring out of your
pockets
like leaves

Robin Wyatt Dunn - Remarriages

break water and pull rain
it's again
all of my love in a fullness

there are two stories in the air
well, there are more
but these are mine
each half of my body
each driving force of rain

thriving and pain
mystical journeys and Los Angeles.

haul the message and cart the rats
we have enough of that
but we'll have more if you bring it

under your hat

over your eyes

the tale now silent

so walk

walk heavier
walk in darkness

Robin Wyatt Dunn - Remarriages

where the glow of the gas station is
like a holy monument
sans jesus and mary

hovering like aliens in space

all Los Angles is an alien

bright and beautiful
haunting permanent death

you die forever here
sweeter than anything

our Aztec ways come closer as the
knife but don't cut
they just keep promising on cutting
closer every night

this is the love of my city
always heavily armed

and made new with each passing day

as armies are made new in the
marching

here is not America but space

infinite
and cruel and bright
like a lover better than any you ever had
who leaves you without a word

Robin Wyatt Dunn - Remarriages

these are scenes of a divorce
from you and me
from me and you
from the life and the end

from the truth

say goodbye

wave bye bye

he loves you still
but you'll never see him again

for he is a father.

Make the music from these sounds
about you
Broken glasses and spit
And the traffic
and the fog against the glass
blurring your eyes

make it a weapon you can keep
under your dress
in case Russians arrive
or Muslims

Robin Wyatt Dunn - Remarriages

or Romans
you'll have it there
ready to kill

kill me with you
as they do in Shakespeare
so I'll remember you
as Lear

stuck on his shoe
and unable to get out.

make love with me for the mark
of the path out

righteous and unafraid
we are no longer us
nor anyone else

we are divorced from us
and each from ourselves
and each from our futures

spent on a wish
over a god
on a sea

Robin Wyatt Dunn - Remarriages

forsoever lightning
four miles out:

the hovering city waits for it, like a
lover

but we have to shutter in,
a noose waiting on the ceiling
that we must not look at.

the government has put it there,
encouraging us,
to die.

like a demon would talk,
whispering of the sweet midnight
under the ground.

this lightning keeps moving back and
forward, over the sky.

reminding us of all of the lightnings
each lightning
making plans for the future

lighting our hollows
for a glimpse of the truth

Robin Wyatt Dunn - Remarriages

the man is a word
hovering around the edge
muttering
showing us faces
hinting at his relationships
his dreams

he is speaking
moving his mouth
hovering around the edges
gesturing
pointing
telling us the things that have
happened to him

he is sad
too much has happened
he is unable to tell everything

nor can we listen to it all

but:

we can see what the man cannot
the sea behind him
and all it has seen
as it gives him to us
from his day

rhyming the words out of his mouth

some terrible voyage
from stars

and the birth
of his berth
of words

Robin Wyatt Dunn - Remarriages

bear the lee
over the way
I would shelter it
under my storm

hear me delay
the righteous ones
under my thorn

I am almost all here
under the midnight day

I'll bear the wasted ones
and the crazies
to the silence on the other side of the
street
I'll bear the near ones
to my breast

bear the lee
beneath my feet
so thunder on my honor for a cutter
or a quarter bark glad and meet the
stream who hungers for a dream
inside my mouth;
no quarter
no quarter:

Robin Wyatt Dunn - Remarriages

be me,
for a day
and be you
for an hour
and we'll set our witching lovers to a test

we'll not be bested
not yet–

inside the shelter of the storm under my skin
no catastrophic winter can summon us
no herdsman may use his code
no year will outlast the groan of the child
inside his nap

- -

"bear the lee" first appeared at In Between Hangovers, Feb. 16, 2017.

limber under the impass
forty thousands tons of revolution
proceeding overhead

here in the quiet
we can watch the air shimmering
prior to the explosion

limber and at ease
we can swing our body out over the
rails
banking east

the engines quiver like the horses for
which they are named
desperate to the meet their end
and the water stop

Robin Wyatt Dunn - Remarriages

now being awake
healds its horror for my luncheon
the prime debate
on the last century
of recorded time

in my stomach

give me the fine debate
and the sweet rain

and I will cheer.

I will cheer for your power
over the emblem of the city
now defeated
now surrendering
to god
or television stations
now obnoxious,
and well-timed,

the theater of peasants
sucking on a rind

and watching the earthworms
wriggle over the cosmos

If I could just set it right. Set it right over the grave of my ancestors; that's what this house is; set the cards right in their castle on the table so I don't have to hear the children or pretend I am still their father.

Now I can be sure that I am not anyone, as a father. As a father I am not even a man, just a sort of petty overlord. Bureaucrat installed in the belfry to ward off ill luck. A kind of effigy.

Abandon All Defenses, all ye Who Enter Here, for I am the Father.

The Ultimate Fiction.

The castle is almost done.

My children are three and five. She's not even technically my wife. Just a girl from the beach that I kidnapped.

"Is that what you did," she says, and kisses me.

Robin Wyatt Dunn - Remarriages

Take it away, for I can defend it no longer. Everything I was is gone but new mes keep popping up; it is identity that is the pain, in whatever form, they must keep emerging, like weather patterns, urgent over the horizon, betokening rain and nightmares and endless sleep.

Robin Wyatt Dunn - Remarriages

send me the news
demoniac and vast

hydrogen bombs
inside the brain

electric fire
around the heart

who makes the stones beating my
feet?

each winter
each season

surrounds my head

Robin Wyatt Dunn - Remarriages

still alive
inside the dream

no improbable course

no huey head

break saturn over the park
and milk my delirium
for all it's worth

Robin Wyatt Dunn - Remarriages

It's a long road home, nor will we be
going there for it no longer exists.

Inside the death of dreams are the
hegemonies of love, intricate ornate
full-fallow and iridescent sprites
ineluctable but so dissimilar the
many shapes and foundries of desire
in our boots still walking:

I love you but the effort grows,
weight behind my eyes, and in my
lower back, over my shins, and
around my arms, holy fire, powerful
sheeple, ineluctable as their
constituent parts, beauteous and
shining:

Tell me it wasn't so, that you were
marked different, that you always
knew what you were doing and did it
proudly and without fear, that you
were a savior, some improbable hero,
some golden god, for us to laugh at:

It would be all right to say.

Well, I will have at it anyway, home
is where the BART is, and though it

Robin Wyatt Dunn - Remarriages

has been destroyed too along with
San Francisco I can dream of them
even as you can, for we are united in
tragedy as we are at no other point in
life; tragedy makes us human.

Give me your hands if we be
frenemies; the plague is righteous
and unafraid, like that golden god
you keep in your heart.

Praise the misery of this life, in its
hideous reflections we are born,
unstoppable, not even if we want to,
subsumed in the firing of our
constable earthward, black and
blistered huge reckoning summons to
regret, mortifying revenge, and love:

Give it all to me as I give it to you,
my knuckles into your mouth.

This knuckle sandwich is the
sweetest thing I can give; and I give it
again, all you American Nazis, and
you're all Nazis, with my heart:

Robin Wyatt Dunn - Remarriages

no death comes easy
that's why it's fun
to watch its approach
creeping up
with a smile
and a set of false teeth

and a waving door it shields over its back

we carry your shield over you
on your walk

Robin Wyatt Dunn - Remarriages

what world is it
whose raiment the will of the earth
and its cousins
drifting by
the mercury and light
benights the day
drifting bright
sunfighting
who heard the man say it was time
for ice cream?

it isn't here
it isn't anywhere
the ice cream is gone
into space

and we shall have to find it
searching every dingbat planet
for our delicious prize

who heard the mercury delight the
rain?

it wasn't me
but I think I know the feeling

underneath the freezer pallet
somewhere beneath the earth

Robin Wyatt Dunn - Remarriages

rage my knight reward
herd the cattle into your sword and
die
the death of the nobility
(in secret)

shuck your clothes and walk naked
into the ravine
for the smoke ceremony
and green

bake the ashes and turn the noose
it's loose
it's rouge

for your cheek:

be meek and turn the crank
be lanky turn your shank
for the ire of the damsel of your eye

not I
not I shall see your merry way
for I'm sighting you in my gunsight
till you get away--

smear your face with gamboge
and bring your sword
for the revolution

now to die
over the rain
take me away

backpack and bones

Robin Wyatt Dunn - Remarriages

now wilt
stay no word
count burns and burnt cities
each your own
those thousand burnt cities inside
you

that fire in your eyes
is still torching more

soon you will be a continent of
holocausts
denuded tundra
shaken alpine heights

stutter out your name
for the recorder

I want to hear it one more time

hand me the grenade for the White House
and for all White Houses

luxurious spendthrifts and Puritan howlers;
soft porn underneath the blanket of god

kablooey and chop suey

marmalade and punk inside my trunk

Robin Wyatt Dunn - Remarriages

hear my epitaph read over the breeze
Sigmund Freud and Morse code
arguing about the summer weather

how hot is it
how cold are your arms

these lights are blurred by your eyes

recite the name of the nameless
underneath the vowels are the dits
and dahs of seasons, tree rings over
your body

rooting
rooting for the sky

Robin Wyatt Dunn - Remarriages

bury burn and bury burn
the burial tonight

liquid fire and delight
the mighty times
under some night city

in our California
death defying and nuts

shake the fire off your shoulders
and summon the night around your
dress

for our blessing of the troops
in the finest of the Caliph's traditions

out of the desert into the kingdoms of
the damned
with sword by sword

implicit herding my goats into the
hovercraft

roaring into the megahertz my only
goal

cleanse the doors of perception

and then cleanse the earth of all of
Anastasia

in her terrible beauty

her grave and terrible beauty under
the neon lights

Robin Wyatt Dunn - Remarriages

we can identify the religion in your
thought
by your tone of voice
a nightmare enunciated carefully in
fricative and diphthong

her religion rubs raw the righteous
energies outside in the dark
whose maw is hungry:

place your hand on the vessel
and repeat after me

[ ]

each maw invites the tomb
over your house
to protect it from onlookers
to watch you carefully
and hear your thought

whose thought is it?
inside your head

Robin Wyatt Dunn - Remarriages

we mark the reason for the week
tattered T shirt
blackened thumb
muddy trail
into your backyard
into your backlife

backlives get no rewards
they just get promoted
through the roof in our secret society
overhead

Robin Wyatt Dunn - Remarriages

bear me
readymade
understood
underwent
undergoing
light
and reason
certainty
and death

bear me
under the wineberry
under the ludicrous thought
of light

hurtful and fantastic
spendthrift and cheesy
gargantuan tan
burning the silence
over my eyes

wear all the red
that you can find

over your arms
with the rest of your naked

Robin Wyatt Dunn - Remarriages

it'll just be you
naked,
with red arms

stupendous
burdened with thought
and obscure relatives

having a thought of a destination

knowing women
and some men
the hurting sound
of the moon
swirling above

tell me the name of the river
and the mark of the sun

so I can gun the thoroughfare with
my smile

each night
spent over the freeway
humming the theme to the
invasion

it goes like this

Robin Wyatt Dunn - Remarriages

"pasta and cheerios
marriage and divorce
lightning and thunder
gods and children
smiling over the fire

"celebrate the insanity of it all
carried over your face like wine

"each black sunrise summons thought
as a wizard his familiar
sharpened to your warrior back
for a trip to Washington or Paris
Persepolis or the Orkneys

burning gasoline and sunshine
with a tail hanging out behind my
legs
made out of fire"

Robin Wyatt Dunn - Remarriages

punish the thought
and harpoon the day
wrest it into the vessel of your dream

no deliverer will come
except the sun

blacken your face
beat your feet against the grass
and scream

Robin Wyatt Dunn - Remarriages

burn well
truer
better
lighter
more fire
over your desk
over your hair
over the street
on the tops of buildings
in the subway
the burning girl
and the burning briefcase

Robin Wyatt Dunn - Remarriages

No easy marriage,
Nor any restitution,
in the blockade of the senses under
the american night.
Step out, and smell the scenery
Pasteboard and gravitas and weed
A steed made out of steel
And my wheel, cut from my wife,
Running wild over my hand.

Our marriage is to one another,
Every tree and rock.
Palpable;
August;
Skewed over the day by the missile
sightings.

Launch with me our thermonuclear
deterrent,
To stop the divorce from reality.
Our bequeathement is rich;
The richest dowry,
A quintessence of poems,
Gnawing out your heart:

Come with me to the barricades of
pixels,
and to our own eyes,

Robin Wyatt Dunn - Remarriages

blinking,
shuddering,
under the white light of our own sun:

Each the inheritor of the government
Armed with the greatest nukes
The largest armies
The mightiest bombs and soldiers
with knives and ropes and saws and teeth
Filled with universities
Marching in time to Mozart themes
and Radiohead timpanis scalding the water of the heart,
Take heed over the lightning for our curse,
Made in lead,
Cut into lead and pushed into the Tiberian walls,
of our slow and silent revolution.

Robin Wyatt Dunn - Remarriages

cut now and
fast
cut me away
from the divinity
of time

cut me away
from the face of god

shove me into an alley
and beat me dead

beat me dead.

break booze and spill the wine
no time can tell the right way to say
goodbye
there is no right way

nor can you really say it

Robin Wyatt Dunn - Remarriages

bend the river right in time
no century can keep its wine from
overflowing
now heat may shrink its barrow
its bones overflow all banks

bend weary and canape
horse thief and fray
my limitless embrace
of pacific pacific

Meander Meander
flash bulb

capture the second per century
when the river is watching
winking back at you

Robin Wyatt Dunn - Remarriages

gloss well and cool the powdery
vents
the howling mad
clit and carpet
curl and clam
cull and cram and cate

dainty cate

harbor and understand
mull and reprimand

move and arm the cloak and strand
over your regret
your arm
the land

make and murder rake and will the
older part of sand
the hand

my love

mash mate and milk the milkly fat
the mendicant and brass
hulk and harrow hide and heat
no beat but the dome of the sky

Robin Wyatt Dunn - Remarriages

Kill well and true
with the knife

he makes the wound river bright
with his blood

slice him open and feed the sharks
and the bark of trees
on who are written words
hegemony and night
boring beetles soughing sighs to sing
the evening out between our fingers

cut him up and pitch him in
tomorrow's another day
and another man
and woman

we're killing all of them
all who done us wrong
so many

one at a time

Robin Wyatt Dunn - Remarriages

Los Angeles is leaving Earth
battery powered
amidst a solar storm
people are putting on their
sunglasses
looking down at their phones
and asking directions to Mars

- -

Los Angeles is leaving Earth
leaving me behind
I can hear it still in my head
asking why it never worked
why didn't we get famous enough?
and why did the hummus never
arrive?

- -

The hummus is arriving outside my
apartment
by messenger
in our beautiful city of messengers
I bow to the delivery boy and give
him his money

Robin Wyatt Dunn - Remarriages

burn white hot
like Rudy
with his gold helmet
so hot he forgot to be Irish

and grew up in Cuba instead
where the BBQ is always fresh
and the sea is always close by

and the whales remember the size of
the burn

Robin Wyatt Dunn - Remarriages

now end
end and deliver
your money or your wife

stand and deliver
your honey or your strife

stand and deliver
your monkey or your knife

give me the poem
you wrote on the toilet
and the band you played with when
you were seven

give me the light

Robin Wyatt Dunn - Remarriages

Now hereabouts we've got this river here
This river she made my cousin come back home.
Now you ain't never seen my cousin.
She's purty.
A shinin moon
You ain't never seen my cousin cause you never been here
Down here in the envelope
Where we pick up trash
And wish our mothers goodnight
I can't say
How long it's been
Since I met you
But I know this

We've got a long way to go before this camel starts talking
And I'm interested in what he has to say.

It's a long way
To New York and back
But not as long as the way to your heart

Robin Wyatt Dunn - Remarriages

That journey has no beginning nor end
And she binds the time to herself
With a terrible fever
Like the jacarandas do the bees
We can't love you like you love us
But we've been there

I can see that river
Even now
In my mind

Robin Wyatt Dunn - Remarriages

enyo
ro ro
ho ho
my fro
freedom pants and waves
summer heat
and sundry sleeps

the beard of the weight
and year

round as a pear
your hair
raucous and unafraid
in the weight
of the sound

In Yellow

I turn

Yellow my art

Under yellow my face

Yellow my hands

This yellow stand

This yellow mind

Yellow my argonauts of gold

Yellow my argentine throne

Yellow my word and groan

To you, my love.

Yellow my righteous tiptoe

To the edge of your star

Yellow my dew

Shuddering over the rim of the gate
of you

Robin Wyatt Dunn - Remarriages

here now
by rail
over coffee
in the morning
my lightning
and your heartache
the medulla of the season
and the reach of the earth

each heart
makes news
in the aftermath of explosions
in the religion of the heart
all expiations are journeys
into one another

the balcony
over the plaza
the leer
of the goat
the long arm
and the majesty
of the revolution

summons all its girth
for the lunch
breaks its bread
and its wind

Robin Wyatt Dunn - Remarriages

for the long march
to epiphany

sing out
this season
for your family
over the globe

and make amends
with the dirt
under your boots
Walt Whitman is watching
wondering
what we are up to

I am watching

the sky turn red

Robin Wyatt Dunn - Remarriages

the thing it is
no melody
nor canyon
nor place of rent
the rule of the word
the thought of the absence
here growing

no one will remember it
for too long
no one can possess it

the winter in summer
and in winter the deeper winter
colder than the sky
it warms the mind
for the work of doing
uttering sleep
shaking the boughs of the trees
the buildings ornery unkept
whispering
whispering words
redeeming use
ringing

the thing of it
harrows fine
focuses the edges

fears the edge
and the world

old thing for dancing
flinging about your knees on
ringing the old butt on
harmony huge but unbecoming
becoming years

Robin Wyatt Dunn - Remarriages

fall long
but soft

I invite thee

whose mad face
shines with absence

melody heroic
but quiet

the door and the doughnut
the old shoe
and the mysterious telegram

oxford scribe
mongol rider
Victorian dancer

hell beast
fuming
sweating
gazing into the crowd

looking for the jump

Care package to Mars

Though this will not reach you in
time
I wanted you to have it

Just a few cassette tapes
And notes on who I've been

Buy an ornament for the tree
I feel we're going to have one again

Robin Wyatt Dunn - Remarriages

I've got something to say but it's too
big

now wilt
stay no word
count burns and burnt cities
each your own
those thousand burnt cities inside
you

that fire in your eyes
is still torching more

soon you will be a continent of
holocausts
denuded tundra
shaken alpine heights

stutter out your name
for the recorder

I want to hear it one more time

Robin Wyatt Dunn - Remarriages

- -

Published in Susan: the journal, April 2017.

Robin Wyatt Dunn's Bio

Robin Wyatt Dunn's parents met at Teton National Park, and he was born there in Jackson. Robin writes and teaches in Los Angeles.

By the same author

Books

Forthcoming, Wine Country, poetry
Black Dove, a novel
City, Psychonaut
Colonel Stierlitz, a novella
White Man Book
Conquistador of the Night Lands
Poems from the War, narrative poetry
Julia, Skydaughter, a novella
Last Freedom, a collection of short plays
A Map of Kex's Face
Fighting Down into the Kingdom of Dreams
Line to Night Island, a novella
My Name is Dee
DEE2
Los Angeles, or American Pharaohs
Sunsborne

Chapbooks

Koreatown
Mary
Hanblečeya
Be Closer for my Burn
Telegrams from X County
A Picnic in England
Drive Thru Poems

Feature Films

A Wilderness in Your Heart
Party Games
American Messenger

www.ingramcontent.com/pod-product-compliance
Lightning Source LLC
Chambersburg PA
CBHW070155080526
44586CB00015B/1997